"Denise VanVliet openly s
guide and help others alor.
expressions of her own learned messages from the Universe are
delivered in an enjoyable and playful style with potent teachings to
inspire a sense of mystery and wonder in all of us."

Jacqueline Anderson LMT, CBS, BSN, MNH

"I recommend this writing for both Mystics, those just discovering
a path, and anyone at various places on that road of awakening. This
three-dimensional earth is a purposeful illusion. Through personal
experiences and historical narrative, Denise very cogently aides
the reader in dissolving the illusory veil people and societies have
built between our lives here and now and the Truth. This is an
enlightening and un-encumbering read."

Doug Clack, Spirit Helper

"It has been said that perception is reality. During the fleeting time
that we wear these bodies, truth can be found in that statement, as
our perceptions of ourselves and all that is around us, help us create
what we deem to be reality. *The Way of the Modern Mystic* may change
your perceptions of Mystics, and/or of yourself, and thereby change
your reality."

Rev Dr Jeff Bentley

"Denise VanVliet has been a funnel for so much 'waking up' in
this lifetime for me! From the first afternoon we spent together,
so many doors have been blown wide open for me in terms of
spirit/psychic/energy awareness, my own 'gifts', and possibilities
of the Universe and how it works. She is definitely a teacher/
partner/friend that I am honored to have in this experience. Do
yourself a favor....let her knock your spiritual block off, and enjoy
the experience of reassembling in the way you are meant to be.
Love and Light!"

Rob Russo

"This is a must read for all that are searching of becoming one."

L'Oreal Pinder LMT, CST

THE WAY OF THE
Modern
Mystic

ONE WHO SEES THE EXTRAORDINARY IN THE ORDINARY

Denise VanVliet

BALBOA.
PRESS
A DIVISION OF HAY HOUSE

Balboa Press books may be ordered through booksellers or by contacting:

Balboa Press
A Division of Hay House
1663 Liberty Drive
Bloomington, IN 47403
www.balboapress.com
1-(877) 407-4847

Because of the dynamic nature of the Internet, any web addresses or links contained in this book may have changed since publication and may no longer be valid. The views expressed in this work are solely those of the author and do not necessarily reflect the views of the publisher, and the publisher hereby disclaims any responsibility for them.

The author of this book does not dispense medical advice or prescribe the use of any technique as a form of treatment for physical, emotional, or medical problems without the advice of a physician, either directly or indirectly. The intent of the author is only to offer information of a general nature to help you in your quest for emotional and spiritual well-being. In the event you use any of the information in this book for yourself, which is your constitutional right, the author and the publisher assume no responsibility for your actions.

Certain stock imagery © Thinkstock.
Any people depicted in stock imagery provided by Thinkstock are models, and such images are being used for illustrative purposes only.

ISBN: 978-1-4525-4765-7 (e)
ISBN: 978-1-4525-4766-4 (sc)

Library of Congress Control Number: 2012903030

Printed in the United States of America

Balboa Press rev. date: 2/28/2012

ACKNOWLEDGMENTS

This project has been a wonderful journey and would not have been possible without the help of those that I have a deep connection to and respect for.

I would like to extend a special thank you to Heather Nelson for her professionalism and her knowledge of the English language with editing this project.

Thank you to Doug and Stacy. I love you both dearly.

Thank you my sweet Kayley for helping with the idea for the cover of the book.

Thank you to everyone that has come into my experience. I love you.

I love you Drew.

DEDICATION

To the person who is ready to peel away the character that is an illusion, and finds the truth within.

May we begin to disrobe the idea that we are separate, let go of beliefs that no longer serve us, and let go of any of the labels that we use to limit ourselves. Open the heart through the senses, and feel the awe for the great mystery - that which cannot be named.

CONTENTS

FOREWORD

I have known Denise VanVliet for a handful of years now, as my companion along the Way of the Modern Mystic. I have acquired a deep respect for her capabilities and her insights. In this book, *The Way of the Modern Mystic*, she shares the insights and perceptions she has distilled into basic core concepts, which I find to be true to my own understandings. I believe what she has written here is a very useful book, that can assist many of the people now Awakening in our time, to make sense of the process and experiences that they are going through, even without the aid of a personal mentor or teacher.

Denise has a talent for taking the concepts of Awakening from the vague mists of ancient teachings and rendering them into today's language and common everyday experiences. In writing this book, she does us all a favor with her talent, for what has seemed to be some rarified state of attainment in the past, which was almost beyond common comprehension, is becoming a topic of discussion and a pathway of experience for people everywhere, at this critical time for humanity in which we need to rise above our previous ways of being, and find an improved approach to expressing our selves and caring for the environment that sustains us all.

In this book, Denise opens the door very wide, so that you too may receive a glimpse into the process of Awakening; and she encourages you to actually step through that doorway, and onto the path, for your own self. Denise offers you reassurance every step of the Way, that you are upon a path that will open up your everyday experience to become something richer, deeper and more meaningful, without asking you to give up all those aspects of your life – family and career – that are so important to you. She shows you how to be in this world as a Modern Mystic, whose expression encompasses both the seen and the unseen worlds simultaneously, and how to do that with grace and ease.

Deborah Hart Yemm

A MOMENT OF CLARITY

This book is about my experiences and realizations from my perspective as a woman. I can only speak from my perspective, which I why I chose to use the pronoun 'she' throughout the book.

This is not a "How-To" book. Am I a Mystic? If I am, that means that you are, too. Am I awakened? If I am, that means that you are, too. For me, there is no "I." I disappeared.

If the words that I use to describe my experiences touch something within you, then that is perfection. If the words that I use to describe my experiences bring out judgment and criticism as to what it means to be a Mystic, and what it means to be awakened, enlightened, or come to realization, then that is perfection.

Inspiration guided me to put these words onto paper. My intention is to bring awareness. Awareness is the path to awakening.

WHAT IS A MYSTIC?

"All the world's a stage, and all the men and women merely players; they have their exits and their entrances; and one man in his time plays many parts, his acts being seven ages."

~ William Shakespeare

Imagine, if you will, that there are three types of people in the world. All of them are involved in a very elaborate production in this grand theater called Earth. There are those who are playing the part of various characters and taking their role very seriously. They actually believe that they are real characters. They identify themselves with every aspect of the character that they are playing. They dress the part and make it seem very real.

Then, there are those in the audience who observe the production. Most people in the audience truly believe that what they are watching is very real. They believe that the people who die in the production, in fact do die. Yet some in the audience may start to realize that what they are observing isn't real.

There also exist those who have been watching for a while, and then realize that what they are watching is a projection. They start to ask a question. "From where is this projection coming?" They start to question everything. They begin to look around and follow that light in the back of the theater, and discover the source of where this very real-looking projection is coming. They get up off of their seats, and begin to leave the theater and head toward the source of the light. It is at this point that they discover something which they, at one point, believed to be true, is really a projection or illusion.

Each one of us plays a very important role in keeping the illusion of this highly elaborate production appearing very real. Only a handful of us will get up, leave the theater, and follow the light to discover the truth.

In my book, *Embrace the BITCH within – Being In Total Connection with Herself*, I talked about the three stages to the process of awakening. Those who were asleep would be the ones in character, participating in this elaborate production and believing that they really are the characters, and that the entire production is real. It is very real to them and you will never be able to convince them otherwise.

Then, we examined those who were in the process of waking up. These individuals would comprise the audience members who are observing the actions that take place before them. They are in between the states of being asleep and waking up. They know that there is something more to this production, but they are not sure what it is exactly. Therefore, they will observe, watch, and pay attention. They may begin to separate themselves from the rest of the characters in the production, wanting less and less to do with what they observe. Some may even completely disassociate themselves from the madness that they are observing while still thinking that what they are observing is real. They believe that there is a reason for everything. Those being the Seekers, the ones searching for answers, will search for deeper meanings than the ones which they can currently see. They will seek God and various spiritual paths. Some are satisfied with what they find, but a handful will feel like there is more to discover.

Then we have those who are fully awake. They are the ones who started to really take a good hard look around and within, and realized that what they were observing in this elaborate production is actually more like a projection. They followed that light and found the source of it. They saw the truth.

A Mystic is someone who took the path to become awakened, and has seen and felt the truth.

The roots of the word *Mystic* can even be found in the Tao Te Ching, as "that which cannot be named."

Anyone with the desire and courage to accept the path of a Mystic is on a path to spiritual realization. There is no magic pill. It requires a lot of internal work to undo the conditioning and programming that has blinded our eyes from seeing the truth. This journey transcends the mind, beliefs, labels, and any identification to this earthy realm. A Mystic knows that he or she is a direct expression of source. They can see that expression all around them and what they see and experience is source as one.

A Mystic is one who sees the extraordinary in the ordinary.

MYSTICS WHO
SHOWED THE WAY

Most religions found around the world will base their entire teaching and philosophy on the Mystic or teacher who taught a handful of disciples or followers the realizations that they have seen. The one with whom most of us are familiar is Jesus. He came to his realization or awakening, and then taught it to his 12 disciples. An entire religion was birthed. Then there was Buddha, who existed about 500 years before Jesus. The Buddha said, "Do not believe in anything simply because you have heard it. Do not believe in anything simply because it is spoken and rumored by many. Do not believe in anything simply because it is found written in your religious books. Do not believe in anything merely on the authority of your teachers and elders. Do not believe in traditions because they have been handed down for many generations. Yet after observation and analysis, when you find that anything agrees with reason and is conducive to the good and benefit of one and all, accept it and live up to it." And yet an entire religion is based on his words, and more people want to become awakened, just like the Buddha.

There are a host of examples of Mystics who came to realizations and then tried to express those realizations into words. To most people, the Mystic seemed to be talking in contradictions or riddles. These misunderstandings of the words have led to taking these realizations and making them into facts or taking them literally. Some religions teach what was originally taught; and then try to live by the words literally. An example would be when Jesus said, "Seek first the Kingdom of Heaven." By taking these teachings literally, many believe that heaven is an actual place that we have to find, or we have to find favor with, in order to enter. Then Jesus said, "The Kingdom of Heaven is within you." This would seem like a contradiction, but again, it's the result of more confusion with the words and taking those words literally. What Jesus did was use the words of his time to express the truths that he experienced. We do not even know his original words. The essence of what he said has gone through interpretations and translations, but when you experience truth, there are no words to express it.

Some of the most amazing Mystics are the ones who expressed their realizations through poetry or art. Rumi, Picasso, Van Gogh, and Walt Whitman are great examples of Mystics who expressed their realizations through art and poetry to get to the heart of the expression instead of the intellect through words. You cannot reach a state of awakening through philosophical thinking, through the intellect, or through logical thinking.

I'm going to repeat that.

You cannot come to a state of awakening through philosophical thinking, through the intellect, or through logical thinking.

STAGES TO AWAKENING

Words can stifle. These are not the only stages to awakening, but just an observation of the stages that many Mystics have experienced. There have been those who experienced instant awakening, so approach this concept with an open mind, without set beliefs and ideas that this is the way it is for everyone. This is an attempt to point one in the right direction. Here is a perfect example of how words can fail. When I say point in the right direction, I'm insinuating that there is then a wrong direction. There is no right or wrong direction. The metaphor example that I like to use is with a picture of a hand pointing to the moon. The hand is trying to direct the person to 'see' the moon. The hand represents the words used, and the moon represents awakening or seeing. Most people will look at the hand and the words, and never see the moon or awaken.

Our true nature is to see. We are all naturally awakened or Mystics. Just like the Buddha said, "We are all Buddhas." So please, take these words with a grain of salt, so to speak. Feel the intention behind them. Create a visual in your mind's eye as to what it would look and feel like. Allow the intention of the words to enter the subconscious and bring forth your own realizations. Don't get caught up in the words. A Mystic will tear down the veils of illusion. She will see the veil within us that prevents us from seeing ourselves. She will tear down the mental constructs of beliefs, fears, and illusions of what we see as reality. She will see that there is no self, and will no longer identify with the self.

All of the world's religions will talk about a sacred journey into which the Mystic will consciously enter. This is not a journey in the physical world, but rather a journey of the inner world. It is a self-annihilation of the beliefs and illusions that we are separate. It is the annihilation of the conditioned and programmed ideas and philosophies within the mind that keep us blind to seeing truth. Many talk about this process and consider it to be killing the ego. Yet really, the ego is just the blanket that we pull over our eyes. The ego is not reality. The ego is a construction that we created to keep the illusion that I am me, you are you, and we are separate, very real. I am here and you are there. Ego is the idea that we are separate. Jesus himself said, "I and the Father are One."

In many of the ancient and sacred writings, the Mystic will enter a process of transformation; cut them self off from the rest of society, and go into the wilderness facing their fears head on. Yet in the 21st century, we don't have much of a wilderness left. We have paved over our gardens and replaced forests with blacktop. The journey that we take today is between the 9 to 5 job, after putting the laundry in the dryer and cleaning up the kitchen after dinner. It may seem impossible to remove ourselves from everyday ways of living and thinking. In the modern world, we go through a process of glimpses of awareness and realizations. It's also what I like to call spiritual experiences. We get a piece of awareness, and then it's back to work. During a night of purging your thoughts, beliefs, and ideas, you come to more awareness and realization. The next day, you are at a gathering with family and friends, and they start to notice a change in you. You start to 'see' things that you had never previously noticed.

Is it possible for a Mystic to *be* in the world and yet no part of it? Indeed!

I have noticed four commonalities that most Mystics possess. First, most spoke about a shift in consciousness. It could be what they call an awakening, a realization, or even being born again.

Second, they may have had an experience of despair. An example would be Jesus traveling in the desert for 40 days, or the Buddha under the Boddhi tree. For many, it was a face-to-face experience with death. That was my experience. I came face to face with my own mortality, a diagnosis of cancer.

The third commonality was an inner journey or a surrendering. A letting go. With this surrendering, comes an annihilation of the self. When the self is shed, an experience of knowing and pure bliss fills the space that the self inhabited.

The fourth commonality that is shared by many Mystics is going into hiding, or becoming a monk or hermit in order to avoid people. This may have happened because they were misunderstood by most people. Jesus is known to have said, "Those who have ears to hear, let them hear, and those who have eyes to see, let them see." Not many had ears and not many had eyes. Because of the misunderstandings of Jesus' teachings, he was put to death, or so the story goes.

Much of the mystical writings point to the awareness that spiritual truth cannot be put into words; one cannot come to awakening through philosophical thinking, through the intellect, or through logical thinking. The only way is to experience.

If I were to describe to you what it feels like to go outside in the middle of winter and pick up snow from the ground, create a snowball, and describe what the snow feels like as I'm packing it together with my hands, I would try to use every detail that I could to help you understand my experience. However, if someone has never experienced winter, snow, or even a good packing snow, words will fall very short of the experience. The person will only have my words to go by. (The hand pointing to the moon.) Yet if the person were to set out on a solo journey and go to a place to experience winter and the feeling of packing a snowball, then the person now has the experience (seeing the moon)!

In our modern world, so many of us currently have this overwhelming feeling of a shift in consciousness, with many of us now on the path to awakening. The first commonality of becoming a Mystic or awakening is this shift in consciousness. Many are now experiencing this. The second is that when we are killing the Earth, we are killing ourselves. We are all coming face to face with death. This is the reason, I believe, why we are in the process of a Great Awakening. Therefore, prepare for the next step. Surrender. Let go. You will experience an annihilation of the self. It is a death experience, but the death of an illusion. If we don't let the self die, we will all physically die. If that is what is happening, then we will come to a point where that is okay. The mass shift in consciousness will then bring all of us to a knowing. We will no longer need any religious or spiritual guidance from outside ourselves, for it already reside within us.

BELIEFS AND STORIES (BS)

The Law of Attraction teachings can be great stepping stones to help you on your journey to awakening. Be aware that some of the teachings seem to be keeping people focused on getting, wanting, and manifesting things in this illusory reality. It is all perfection. One teacher of the Law of Attraction is teaching this idea of creating a story. For example, if you had a bad experience in the past, then you would be creating a different story so that you could change your emotions that are attached to the story. Raise your vibration when you recreate the story in your mind. I can see how this concept is designed to help people understand that the story that they've held onto can be changed in an instant, if they so choose. These stories that they've held onto, sometimes for a lifetime, are illusions, no longer real, but what is happening is that people are misunderstanding and still holding onto a story. They are so emotionally attached to their stories. They identify themselves with the story, such that when they repeat it again and again to themselves and others, it is as if the story is who they are. I've heard people say that they play the tapes over and over again in their heads. They are filling their heads with *beliefs* and *stories*, also what I lovingly call BS.

For some reason, the brain or mind loves stories. It stimulates the imagination. We will have an experience and then tell the story of it over and over again. If we have an emotional experience, what happens in the body, on a chemical level, is that the body then experiences the event over and over again as if it is happening right now. Have you ever listened to someone tell a story, and witnessed this individual get all excited or stressed out, depending on the content of the story? The body is reliving this event as the story is told, every single time.

A perfect example of the body experiencing what the brain is retelling is sex. After having an orgasmic experience of sex, one can relive that moment over and over again in the mind. Just thinking and reliving that experience in the mind, the body starts to respond. If the person keeps thinking about it long enough, the body responds with an orgasm. Imagine that!

Experiences are part of the reason why we come to this three-dimensional realm. All of the experiences that we have are perfection. All of them. The separation comes when we label this experience as good, and that experience as bad. When someone is awakened, they can see that all experiences are perfection.

Pain and pleasure reside in the same area of the brain. For an experience that some might label as bad or painful, others might label as good or pleasurable. A perfect example would be the idea of eating dogs or horses. In the United States, those actions are labeled as very bad, and just the idea of eating our family pet is painful. However, in other countries, eating a dog or horse is considered a delicacy, is delicious, and even enjoyable.

The mind is either in the past or the future. The body is always in the now. This is a very important point to realize. The mind is either in the past or the future, and the body is always in the now. The body does not understand that the mind is reliving something from the past or dreaming of something into the future. The body only knows right now.

The reason why affirmations or spells will work, for the most part, is because they are stated in the now. If you state an affirmation such as, "I will stop smoking," you are making a statement for some time in the future. In order to connect the mind to the body, you must say the affirmation in a language that the body understands. "I am an ex-smoker." It is done. I love the example of the sign on the bar entry door that says, "Free beer tomorrow." You can keep coming everyday and never get your free beer, making a need to work *with* the body, as its own consciousness, necessary.

The mind is never in the now. The mind/ego only knows the past or future. It takes experiences of the past, and bases what those experiences were on what it could be like in the future. That experience was good, so I would do that again. That experience was bad and I should avoid it in the future. Awakening is in the now. That's why there is mind/ego bashing and killing going on these days. Yet, why would we want to kill something that is natural to us, and even needed in this realm? We need mind/ego in this dualistic reality. Think of the mind/ego as the costume that you are wearing for this magnificent theater production called Earth. We just need to train the mind/ego to work for us, and not let it be the other way around. Most people, however, don't have the time, patience, or know-how to train the mind/ego. They want a quick fix. Just kill it! This is the thinking that we see in many aspects of our lives. We get sick; we go to the doctor for a pill. We want health; we go to the health store for a pill. Killing the ego is a quick fix 'pill.' We have an instant-gratification mentality, but just killing the mind/ego is not going to bring awakening. Awakening is recognizing that you are not mind/ego. That's it!

Challenge any beliefs and stories (BS) onto which you hold. One thing you can do, if you so choose, is set aside one evening a week and do what I call "purge on paper." If, during the week, you discover some beliefs onto which you currently hold, just write them down. If you observe things that you can't stand or hate in other people, take note of those things. That is a great place to start. The people or things we hate the most, or react to the most, are our best teachers. During your purge-on-paper night, puke-up these beliefs and observations on paper. Write them down, and then ask yourself from where they came. What I have found is that most of the time, the beliefs that we have were given to us. If you find yourself telling a story over and over again, start to pay attention to how your body is responding. Write the story down and then leave it on the paper. Share your experiences without the emotional attachment to them so that the body doesn't respond as if the experience is happening right now. Just being aware of them is the way to awakening.

Choose your beliefs and stories wisely. Choose to hang on to the BS or let it go. You always have the choice. The word *belief* is an interesting contradiction. Within the word itself is the word *lie*. *"Be'lie'f."* If you can touch it, taste it, hear it, see it, and smell it, then it must be true, right? These senses are deep inside in the dark parts of the brain. We 'see' at the back of our brain, which is called the occipital lobe. Seeing does not happen with the eyes. The eyes transfer vibration or light to the back of the brain, and that dark blind area 'sees' or interprets our external world. You can believe that your eyes see the world, but is what you see true? What we see is a projection. It's just like the analogy of the movie theater. What we see comes from the back of the theater or the back of the brain. It's all perfection.

With that in mind, get out of your head. Use less mind/ego, feel more in the body and practice thinking with the heart center. Stop anal-yzing and retelling the same old beliefs and stories (BS). Just *feel*. The body will reveal the ultimate in consciousness. This awakening of consciousness is not in the mind.

WHAT'S LOVE GOT
TO DO WITH IT?

Love. I looked up this word in the dictionary one day, and it basically says that love is a profoundly tender, passionate affection for another person. Love is a feeling of warm personal attachment or deep affection for another. It can also be sexual passion or desire.

In our three-dimensional, dualistic reality, most of us really don't know what true unconditional love really means. Most of the definitions that I looked up for the word love showed conditional love. As long as there is tender, passionate affection for another person, there is love. Yet as soon as said tender, passionate affection turns to something else, the love can become hate. When the love that is a feeling of warm, personal attachment or deep affection for another becomes its opposite, look out! Also, when the love is sexual passion or desire and that passion and desire are gone, what then remains?

Most of us know love in the dualistic linear fashion. We have love at one end of the stick and hate at the other. Isn't it easier to hate the ones you love the most? Love for a partner is strong, but as soon as he or she cheats on you, it instantly becomes hate. Can you unconditionally love your partner even if they have cheated on you?

The love that most of us are taught is either linear or conditional. When someone behaves toward us in a way that we like, we show them love. When they don't behave in the way that we like, we withhold our love. We can also use guilted love. "If you loved me, you would _____ (fill in the blank)." Guilt is a strong motivator to force someone to do what we want, but is that really love?

When you hear the word love, what does it do to you? What happens in your body? What memories come up for you? There is an awful lot of baggage tied to that four-letter word. Just love, for love is what makes the world go round. All you need is love…blah blah blah.

I've read a lot of the New Age stuff, and it all talks about this love, but what exactly is it that they are talking about? It's not the linear, dualistic type of love with which we are all too familiar. Yeah, the stick thing; love on one end of the stick and hate on the other. This feeling of unconditional love is something that comes from within us and within everything. When we tell someone that we love them, it's not that person who we actually love. It's the feeling that they invoke within us that we love. Knowing that, do you really need the person to have that feeling? Do we really need to depend on someone to allow that feeling to come from the inside out? We are all so addicted to getting that feeling from outside of ourselves. It's a fix. We need that outside stimulation to feel love, but that doesn't make it real love. That is conditional love. Men are taught to find someone who completes them. Women are taught to find a man to take care of them. This is love...with an ulterior motive!

To me, true love is actually this substance that flows through everything. You can call it the no-thing, you can call it God or consciousness, or you can call it the light. This substance can be compared to asking a fish about the water in which it lives. The fish would answer with, "What water?" Even though the water is what sustains and connects it to everything in the ocean, in its world, it doesn't *see* the water. If someone from another dimension were to come to our world and ask us about the ether substance in which we live, we would ask, "What are you talking about?" We can't see, smell, feel, taste, or touch it. And yet there still is something there. That something would be the love! That is the thing. It's just like fish in the ocean, which sustain and connect us to everything. Therefore, we have linear conditional love, which is love on one end of the stick and hate on the other, and then we have love in a circle, which is defined as there being no end and no conditions.

From a Mystic's view, or when a person awakens, she sees this stuff everywhere! It's oozing from the plants, animals, and people. Yes, even the people, who at one point couldn't be tolerated. It's mind blowing. Many who awaken will write about just being in a bliss state for a year or more after their realization. It is just awe inspiring. There are no words to describe it other than perpetual spiritual orgasm. When you awaken to this feeling, you are in bliss. It's more than love. It's one more letter than love, so it's not a four-letter word at all, and there is a lot less baggage tied to the word *bliss*. Whenever I think about my experience of disappearing, after surrendering to the horror of the self disappearing, I remember that I was in a state of bliss. I became one with everything. Everything and everyone was me. I was the experience of the tree, the dog, the weed, and the old lady crossing the road. There was/is no separation. That is pure bliss, much deeper than the limited idea of love. Then again, the word bliss is an idea too. Pick the word that resonates with you. It really doesn't matter what word you choose. You can call it whatever you want, as long as it is the feeling that expands from the inside out. It's not the feeling that you think someone else gives you. Can you feel the difference? That is awakening!

So the word love has a pretty bad rap. Love is the addiction that we crave for someone to give us that feeling. Bliss is what is already inside, and most of us have never felt it. This love is the same as source. It is not a verb. It's not something that you *do*; it's something that you *be*.

I love visuals. The love that most of us know is linear. We've already talked about the first visual; we imagined a stick, linear. At one end of the stick is love, and at the other, opposite end, is hate. The visual from a Mystic's point of view is that there is just love. A circle, love is the energy, consciousness, or source that flows through you and everything, even the stick. Love is right here, and we get to choose how much of it is going to flow through us at any given moment.

The second visual that I love is that of a garden hose. The physical hose represents the physical body. The water running through the hose represents the source energy, or love. We get to decide how much source energy we allow to flow through us. That is free will. When we have beliefs, ideas, rigid thinking, thoughts of not being worthy or hate of ourselves, and ideas or philosophies that are followed literally when they are meant to be used metaphorically, this will pinch off the garden hose and limit how much source love can flow through it.

The more that you allow love to flow through you, the more that you will awaken. The more that you come to see that you are me, I am you, and we are no-thing, the more that you will awaken. The love that is flowing through me is flowing through my dogs, the trees, the guy that just cut me off on the interstate, the mass murderer, the president, Hitler. This is the reason why those who are awake say that all of us are already awake. We get to decide how much we pinch ourselves off from allowing all that is to flow through us! If you could just un-pinch yourself, you will see that you are already awake.

Do you think that it's possible to love a mass murderer or someone like Hitler? Most, actually more than 99% of us will say, "No way in hell!"

Yet when you awaken, you will see the love that flows, even through those people, because you realize that you are those people! Now, do you really want to be a Mystic?

DO YOU REALLY WANT
TO BE A MYSTIC?

Just as some people would rather not go to the doctor to find out why they are having health issues for fear that it's something serious, some people might not want to really see and awaken to all that is. That is just fine. There is no right or wrong. Some would just rather be right where they are. That is perfection.

I set out on a journey to awaken. It seemed to be something that was already in me. I do remember that when I was a kid, I went to go see a movie with my Aunt. I really wasn't into the movie that much, and found myself looking around the theater and watching other people watching the movie. I think I was about 9 or 10 years old. I remember looking up at the ceiling of the old theater. Some of the old theaters in Chicago had some of the most magnificent architecture. Then, I noticed little dust particles floating near the ceiling and saw that they were coming from the light of the projector that was playing the movie. I followed them, and they led to this tiny square hole in the wall, way behind us and near the ceiling. The point? Even at age 9 or 10, I was in the audience, so to speak. Looking back when I was a kid, I was probably already in the second stage.

Once someone sets out on this journey, there seems to be a strong pull to reach the end. It used to be a very lonely journey, but today, it seems like many are on this path. Is it this shift in consciousness that everyone is talking about? Maybe. Either way, it feels like people are so spiritually starved now that they are ready for the shift. The more that people awaken, the more that other people will awaken because the ones before them chose to be awakened. It's almost like a group phenomena thing going on right now. Either that, or I'm just talking in circles.

Some individuals try to stop the process because it can be very frightening. Some symptoms of awakening are fear, anxiety, panic attacks, and depression. It's not always the joyful, bliss-filled experience that some people talk about it being. The mind has thoughts that are everywhere, and the body is responding with elevated adrenaline and cortisol. The first reaction is to do something to stop this overwhelming feeling. The more that we try to do something, the worse that the awakening symptoms get. Remember the garden hose analogy? When you pinch yourself off of the water, source, which is flowing through you, you cause a great deal of pressure to build. The best thing to do is just be with the feelings. Don't *do* anything. Just *be*. This is what the Buddha did. He just sat with his fears without trying to do anything with them, and then they were gone.

Here is another question to ask yourself. Are you ready for the self to die? Before I had my realization, I had a dream. In my dream, I was a drop of water. The ocean was calling me back home. I didn't want to go back and I was arguing with the ocean, saying that I was different from all of the other drops of water. Imagine a little red-headed girl stomping her feet and trying to get her way with the ocean. I was explaining that I had special gifts and talents that were different from all of the other drops of water. The ocean would have nothing more to do with my petty explanations and swallowed me up. In that moment of my dream, I was overcome with fear, dread, elation, bliss, and oneness. I was all of the other drops in the ocean. I was the ocean! There was no more me. There was just ocean.

Perhaps this dream prepared me for my realization. A few months after that dream, while in meditation, the self got swallowed up in all that is. I started to feel fear while falling into an empty space, the void. I decided to let go of the fear, surrender, so that the Universe could show me what I needed to see. In that moment, there was no more me. There was just oneness. I was everything and everything was me. I disappeared. It was the most terrifying, blissful experience I've ever had.

Now I see other people differently. They are me. Yes, this includes people who cut me off in traffic, along with mass murderers like Hitler. How is that possible? Compassion.

COMPASSION

I've heard the Dalai Lama talk about compassion and read the Buddhist teachings about compassion, and even Jesus spoke about loving your neighbor and your enemy as yourself. Most people will say, "Sure, I have compassion. It's a type of love, right?"

In linear or dualistic thinking, (yeah the stick thing) it's easy to have compassion for the people you love. Yet with this type of linear love, how on Earth can anyone have compassion for someone like Hitler, or the terrorists who took down the Twin Towers, or the enemy with which we are at war? It's not possible to even come close to anything like compassion with dualistic love.

One definition of compassion is to "love your neighbor as yourself." Do we really *know* our neighbors? Most of us don't even have love for the self, so how is it even possible to love another? How about, "Love your enemy?" How is it possible to love an enemy? Enemy is on the same side of the linear stick as hate.

It is possible, but there is no easy way to say it, and the words are really going to make it easy to misunderstand. Here it is: I *am* Hitler, and I *am* the terrorists who took down the Twin Towers, I *am* the enemy. Please do not take this literally. I am trying to use limited words to explain something that cannot be explained. There is only one consciousness.

Today, you will hear and read about the light, and that the light is good. It will also mean that there is an opposite. In dualistic linear thinking, that would mean that the dark is bad. How is it possible to have compassion for bad or for darkness?

The Mystic embraces the darkness. Without darkness, there is no light. She embraces the feelings and fears that most of us suppress, the things that we don't want to be, and what we are afraid of becoming. Start to embrace those things about yourself. We all have the dark within, that dark self; embrace that part of yourself so that you know who you really are. When we suppress these parts of our self, we are really not embracing our complete self. We all have issues and things that we don't like about ourselves, but as soon as we embrace that part of our self, we see everyone within us. We see our self within everyone. This is who we are: dark and light. Without light, there is no dark. Without dark, there is no light. Being aware of the fears that build within and allowing those fears to just *be* instead of suppressing them, lets us feel other people's fears. Their fears are our fears. Consciousness is freely flowing through us.

Let's get back to how anyone can have compassion for someone like Hitler or the terrorists who did what they did. If I had their experiences, fears, thoughts, ideas and beliefs, could I have done what they did? Maybe. At the time, Hitler truly believed that he was doing the right thing for his country and people. He truly believed that he was being Darwin-scientific about it and that he was doing what was right. I also have compassion for all of the people who died because of his beliefs. The experiences are perfection. It was and is a perfect manifestation of consciousness. Consciousness does not have a sense of what is right and wrong. That comes from our linear thinking and mind. Again, please don't misunderstand. I am not saying that what happened was right or wrong. It was a manifestation of consciousness in its perfection.

I can feel the energetic walls going up because of the words not being able to express the true nature of what cannot be expressed in words, and the misunderstandings because of the emotional charges to these experiences. The Mystics of the past taught similar ideas with limited words, and people misunderstood and followed the words as literal. Let me ask; can you find the darkness within you? Can you find the terrorist within you? That part of you that you hate inside of yourself? What we think we hate outside of ourselves comes from within. Connect with that part of you so that you can have compassion for those who allow this part of themselves to be expressed as their truth.

I'll give a lighter example. I hated lying, and I hated liars. I thought it was something that other people did. It was morally wrong. I was not a liar, but it seemed like I attracted liars into my experience all of the time. As part of my realization, I embraced the liar within myself, the dark part of me that I was suppressing. I am a liar. I am that which I hate. Once I had that awareness, I was able to feel the liar within, feel when others were lying, and feel the liar within them. I was then able to have compassion for the person because I could feel the hate that they felt for themselves when they were in the act of lying, or I could feel the denial within them as they were convincing themselves into believing that they were actually telling the truth.

Start on a smaller scale by finding those things that you hate in other people and find that dark part within yourself. Tell yourself, "I am that which I hate." Feel that part of yourself and just be with it. Then, when you come across someone who showed you that part of yourself that you hated, you will feel compassion for that person because you *are* that person.

The only enemy that compassion has is fear. Fear closes us off from being able to see clearly. When we are full of fear, it disengages our resilience or the ability to bounce back. Just take a look around you right now. Our society is full of fear. We've had setbacks in the past. Take a look back at our history. This time though, people are so full of fear that they do not see a way out, and there is no resilience or ability to bounce back.

On a physical level, it has been shown that compassion enhances our body's immune system. But what exactly is compassion? Very few of us truly know the definition of compassion. I looked up the word *compassion* in the dictionary, and it basically says that it's *sympathy*. I feel like compassion goes well beyond sympathy. From a Mystic's view, here is how I see it. Compassion is a perception. To me, it means taking on the vibration of suffering from another person as my own, and then transforming that energy into love. This transformation of the energy is the beginning of healing. It's *com*-plete *passion* for another sentient being as my own. I am them, and they are me.

If I have no compassion for myself, I can have no compassion for another sentient being.

Start with compassion for yourself. Notice the internal dialogue that you have within your own mind. Starting with yourself is the bridge to having compassion for others.

NO LINES, JUST CIRCLES

I'm a very visual person, and sometimes, pictures will pop into my head. Depending on your awareness, the source energy that flows through you will use whatever sense is strongest within you. Mine is vision.

The picture that I saw was a circle, and in the very center of the circle was death or the nothingness. The outside parameter of the circle is life. Most of us see life and death as linear opposites. On one end of the stick is life, and on the other end is death. With dualistic thinking, this makes perfect sense, but if you really examine how life works, it goes in cycles. They can be cycles of the seasons: spring, summer, fall, and winter. The cycles of the moon, a cell, and an atom all represent a circle, not a linear line. There is no beginning or end. There is no alpha or omega.

Therefore, you begin to go inside, into that space, feel that nothingness or that darkness that is our center, or what some Mystics call "The Void". That is where most of us are afraid to venture. We think that there is nothing there. Well, there *is* no-thing there. It feels more like we are afraid that we *are* nothing. The self cannot enter this space, for if it does, it will become annihilated. When you are in the process of awakening and you connect to that center, to that nothingness, you begin to realize that there is no separation. You are that.

"I am that I am."

Many are familiar with that statement from the Bible in Exodus 3:14 "I am that I am." However, if you add a comma, it's amazing how it can change the entire meaning of a sentence. Look at the following sentence.

"Let's eat Grandpa!"

Add a comma, and it changes the entire meaning.

"Let's eat, Grandpa!"

Add a comma to "I am that I am." What do you get?

"I am that, I am."

When you begin to see this world, this grand theatrical production, remind yourself that you are everything. When you are looking at something that you don't like, remind yourself, "I am that, I am." We are everything that is around us. We are the things that we don't like. When we allow something that we don't want or don't like and we let it just *be* in our center, without trying to *do* anything about it, we then are able to release that energy to the outer edge of our center.

When we allow death, it is in that moment that we really live. Most of us are very much afraid of death, or deathly afraid of death. Just the idea of death freezes us or a feeling of terror overcomes us. Some are so afraid of dying that they never actually live. A Mystic can see that there is no death. In the physical sense, a plant grows, then goes back to the Earth so that by the next season, the plant can grow. Even our cycle of breath is an experience of life and death. As we inhale, we breathe in prana, life force. As we exhale, we experience that death or release part of the breath cycle. Death is a release. Our very first breath is an inhale, and our very last breath is an exhale, a complete cycle. We are experiencing life and death with every breath cycle. If you examine how most of us currently breathe, you may notice that you inhale more than you exhale. This imbalance in the breath can cause stress to elevate in the body. If you focus on your exhale, the inhale will happen without any effort on your part. Embrace all of the cycles of life and death that we experience.

NOTHING NEW
UNDER THE SUN

There is absolutely nothing new. There are no new thoughts. There is nothing to fix, nothing to save, nothing to pursue. What we can do is have a different way of looking at it. Awakening is having a different perspective of ordinary, everyday things.

The only guarantee that we have is that nothing stays the same and that everything stays the same. There is this constant ebb and flow of life seeking death, and from death consuming life. Is life hungry for death or is death hungry for life? Without life, there is no death. Without death, there is no life. Awakening is *seeing* that everything is a perfect contradiction. As soon as we have a belief in one side or the other, we are now in dualistic linear thinking. When you see that both are correct or both are illusion, you *see*, you awaken.

Many of the sacred writings come from a language that is no longer used. We have a very different modern world these days. Yes, I have an iPhone, the greatest device of the day. It is a blessing and a burden. Can we still say that space is the final frontier? We now know more about the electron, proton, and neutron. We study the physics of all of them in great detail. Yet these material things do not work without the space in between that gives the cells their power. It's not the cell, it's the space. It is the no-thing. It is the empty space, for that is where the power lies.

Some will ask me, "Who is your guru?" The word *guru* means teacher. I guess you could say that I've had a lot of teachers, not just one. But from my realization, I did not need a guru. Actually, from what I've experienced, a guru can inhibit someone from their own realization.

Generally, a guru is someone who is enlightened. There are many out there that market enlightenment and will sell a program, and if you follow their ways, you too will become enlightened. It's a trap. It's maya. It's perfection. The guru may have a lot of head knowledge, but they don't have the oneness. There is something about a person that you can feel. There is something there and what you feel is within you. There are gurus who have studied the sacred texts, may be very knowledgeable, and developed a following, and they have made their followers pretty much worship the guru.

I once went to a group meditation and the leader of the meditation couldn't start until the picture of his guru was set on the altar first before we could proceed. It took everything in my being to not laugh out loud, but this was his belief! This is not going to bring you to awakening. This is going to make you a follower and fill your head with beliefs and ideas, stuff. If it feels good, then do it, but know that this is not going to make you awakened. It's not the magic pill.

Anyone who is an enlightened being knows that there is nothing to worship. There is nothing. Any kind of worshipping is an indication of separation. You have the deity, God, or guru, and you have yourself. You are separate. If you have seen the truth, you know that there is no separation. You are. I am.

With a guru, the visualization that I had was of somebody in another person's brain mixing spaghetti, twirling it with a fork, and playing with the person's brain. It can be summed up as keeping people in their heads and on traditions, writings, what this means, and what that means. None of it means anything. That is the illusion. Even this book can keep you in your head and focused on the words. I am no guru, for I am just sharing my experiences. My intention is to spark something within you to get you to look at the moon, not at my words or my experience. Experience for yourself.

If you prefer to work with a guru, then that's great! It is up to any person to have a guru or not. It's not wrong if that is the path that you choose. I've studied Christianity, Buddhism, and various beliefs, but it was only when I let go of the beliefs that I really started to open myself up to the oneness and allowed truth to flow through me rather than what was in my head.

I think, "Kill the guru! Kill him!" I would do this in my mind, not literally. You don't need to follow anyone or anything. Don't follow anything that I've said. I share my experiences and observations, but I am no guru. Discover for yourself, as it has to come from the inside. Awakening does not come from the outside, ever. It cannot come from any one teaching. If you look at those who have awakened, you will find an array of religious upbringing and study. The Buddha studied various forms of teachings in his day. Jesus was brought up in the Hebrew teachings and traditions. It was not the religious beliefs and study that led to enlightenment, it was letting go of the religious beliefs that led to awakening. Awakening only comes from the inside; never a person, book, or practice.

NOW WHAT?

Okay, so you had your experience. You disappeared and experienced oneness, experienced the annihilation of the self, and saw the truth. Now what?

"What the hell do I do now?"

There is no going back. You can't take back what you've seen and experienced. You saw the man behind the curtain; you can't just close the curtain, so to speak.

History shows that at one time, the awakened one became a hermit or a monk. There was no way that one could mingle with such dead, asleep, illusory people without going mad; otherwise, the people would somehow have the awakened person killed because they were misunderstood. Off to the hills and away from society was the answer. They would write, create or just exist until their days were up in this illusory universe.

In the modern world, more and more people are coming to realization. We may even work with someone everyday who has come to realization!

I experienced realization between my 44th and 45th birthday. It was a year of rollercoaster rides. After my realization, everything was bullshit; everything! Someone told me that I was starting to sound like some guy who came to realization and wrote about how the universe was haunted. I started feeling myself go down this same path. I had the spiritual annihilation and was starting down a path of physical annihilation. Nothing was real. There was no this, there was no that, there was no you, and there was no me. None of this was here. Nothing existed. It was a big cosmic joke. It was one illusion. It was a path that I started down, and I realized that I had a choice. I could keep going down this path and isolate myself from the illusion that I saw, or I could play.

The Mystic takes another path. A Mystic sees and feels the truth and it instead of saying that it's all bullshit, which is what I started to do, a Mystic will see something that we all normally see, but from a different angle, and then try to put words to it. We are here, and that is the illusory reality of it. Whether or not it is real is another thing.

Consciousness is projected in this realm. What do we do? We can get up on stage, recreate the mind/ego, put on the costume, and play the part and play it "as if." As if, for example, could be, "As if I get the Oscar or I win the reward at the end of the game." Ah! The game! The part! There is no Oscar or award, but there is the fun! Let's play! I realized that I could put back on some kind of costume in order to function in this illusory world. I could put back some beliefs and ideas in order to participate and function in this three-dimensional reality.

There are some choices for people who awaken. There is always a choice. From my observation, it feels like being a Mystic is a path of really trying to touch others and open up their minds to awareness. In the modern world, Eckhart Tolle is one such person. He talks about being in the now, one simple thing that most of us are not able to do. He could easily talk about how there is nothing, why bother being in the now, and how we only have the now. Instead, he chooses to bring people to an awareness of the now. Each person who has experienced the void, the nothingness, the no-thing, has a choice to make. Do you see your awakening as a gift or a curse? This is a dualistic reality. Pick a side, but know that the other side is true as well.

Some people will scare others and tell them the horror of the annihilation of self, but you are only looking at one side of the experience. Yes, there is the horror, but then there is also the bliss, the experience of oneness. Seeing is a whole host of contradictions that beautifully connect and create circles. You have one thing, but you also have the other thing, because it is one thing.

A Mystic will see the connections and contradictions and put beautiful words to the experience, like the 13th century poet Rumi did, to speak to other people through the heart, and hopefully open them up as well. The other path is the one in which they talk about how it's all illusion, there is no afterlife, and there is no higher self. That's really not helping others who are seeking to open up to the possibilities of nothing. They are playing the role of the dragon, the gatekeeper. That is just from one perspective. There is only one perspective, but your experience, my experience, everyone who experiences the void, can see it through the different eyes of the same lens, and can see it through different angles. However, there are no different eyes and there are no different angles. They are all right. You cannot force it. You cannot force awakening. It's up to you. You can put on the costume and play the role or isolate yourself and consider it all an illusion and nothing more. Both are illusory. I choose to have fun with it.

WALL CLIMBING

Does religion play a role in the awakening process? Many follow a form of religion and expect their religion to wake them up, such as Buddhism or Hinduism; the ultimate goal of the religion is to awaken or become enlightened. The problem that I experienced was that I had a head full of useless beliefs and ideas. I had ideas, knowledge, and sacred writings; what I thought was preparing me for awakening. Then, I realized that all I had to do was purge my mind of all of that. You do not need to have any kind of religion, follow a guru, or have any kind of sacred teachings to wake up. As a matter of fact, those things can and will hinder you from waking up. It's okay to study these things, but never study these things as truth. That is not truth. What these teachings will do is give you something to hang on to as you're trying to go into the nothingness. You cannot have anything to hang on to when you are falling into the void and annihilation.

Have you ever seen or climbed one of those indoor, fake rock-climbing walls? I used to take my kids to them and watch as they tried to get to the top without making a mistake and having to start over. Just imagine that each of those hand and foot grips on the climbing wall represents a belief or idea onto which you hang, and they prevent you from falling into the void.

When you are ready to go into the void or into the nothingness, you must let go and not hang on to anything. Everything, every belief, every idea, everything that you have ever learned needs to be questioned, challenged, and let go of in the mind. The mind needs to be stripped naked to nothing in order to go into the void. Then, when you are nothing, there is nothing available for you to fasten your grip, and you are then able to go to the center of nothingness. Be prepared for the self to be annihilated, but also for the blissful feeling of oneness and the knowingness. Know that you are nothing and you are everything. That is the thing with seeing and waking up. Everything becomes a beautiful contradiction because everything is true and nothing is true.

There are all kinds of processes out there to help you challenge your beliefs and ideas. I love *The Work* by Byron Katie. If you are willing to put forth the effort and go through your beliefs and ideas, the rewards are amazing. *The Work* is just one of the many processes out there. You do not have to follow anyone's process. You can make up your own. The idea is to *do* the work. It took time and conditioning to hold onto the beliefs and ideas that you have. It's going to take some work to undo the programming.

PRACTICE MAKES IMPERFECT

I t is the imperfection of the wood that gives the guitar its perfect tone.

How many times have you heard or read that you must practice meditation or some other techniques in order to attain enlightenment? Practice is in the mind. When doing anything with the idea of practice and perfecting, you are entertaining the mind. Mind only.

There are hundreds of forms of meditation and they are all good. I've tried many of them. Find one that feels good to you, and then instead of practicing it, play with it. Practice is the mind and play is experience. Feel the difference? When you practice, you have an expectation. You expect to someday wake up using this technique that you have been faithfully practicing. When you play, you have no expectations, but rather a feeling of wonderment. What can the universe show me today? Let go of the programming of what you think it is or what it should be. Look as if for the first time through the eyes of a child.

When my son first started learning music at about the age of 10, in addition to the practice that his teacher would give him, I would give him a piece of music to listen to and I'd ask him to tell me what the music was telling him. These lessons were teaching him how to interpret music. One day, when he was about 14, I decided to give him a nontraditional piece of music to see what he would tell me. I gave him *The Star-Spangled Banner* by Jimi Hendrix. He listened to that piece for weeks. Because my son was learning the guitar, I felt that feeling the music and expressing himself through music was an important part of becoming a musician. It was not just a matter of being able to read music and repeat a piece perfectly, but without feeling. To me, music is a vibrational representation of emotions.

One day, he was listening to the piece and I could see him trying to figure out in his head the meaning of the song. I interrupted his listening and said:

"Don't think honey, *feel*."

A couple of days later, he came to me and said:

"Mom, I get it! The guitar is *crying!*"

What many people interpret with that piece of music is that playing *The Star-Spangled Banner* imperfectly is a way to defy the government and make a political statement. That may be true. But if you *feel* the music, your emotions and your body will feel the perfection of each note as an outcry that Jimi expressed for the many senseless deaths that occurred during the Vietnam War. The imperfection was a perfect expression of emotion.

Let go of practice. Let go of trying to be perfection. Let the imperfection and play open you up to the possibilities. That is perfection.

INSIDE OUT

Most people have the sense that their outer world is real or objective. It can be measured and tested with a scientific method. They also think that their inner world is illusory or subjective. It cannot be measured or tested. A Mystic sees it as the opposite. The outer world is illusion and the inner world is reality. Your inside world is your reality. Your outside world is a projection of your inner reality. However, you can't mix both of them together because you live in both environments at the same time. They have to be separate, and yet they are one. It is this turning-inside-out process that can cause problems for people in the midst of their own awakenings. At times, there can be confusion, anxiety, and health issues that manifest because of this inside-out phenomenon. It is a complete shift in perspective.

For example, some people talk about the Kundalini waking up. Kundalini is a powerful energy that can lie dormant at the base of the spine, and when awakened can cause heart palpitations, or other, sometimes serious, health issues. During the process of awakening we are getting our inner reality mixed up with our outer world as we awaken. We see what is going on as reality, when in fact it's an illusion because our worlds are going inside out. What's inside becomes the reality, and what is outside becomes the illusion.

We see this principle now with many teachings. The Law of Attraction, for example, teaches that your thoughts become your reality. Most people will see this teaching as your thoughts being the illusion and what manifests as reality. However, this is a wonderful stepping stone on your way to going inside out. From a Mystic's point of view, what is going on inside is reality, and what manifests is illusion. Everything in the outside world is a projection of what is happening inside.

A seeker will be forever looking outside of oneself for enlightenment. They will look to someone who has become enlightened and think that their way is the only way. Yet the person whom they are looking at for enlightenment will have put back on some of the beliefs and ideas, and create a costume in order to participate and function in this three-dimensional illusory reality after experiencing their own enlightenment. This is perfection. Therefore, don't look to someone who has awakened and observe what they are doing now. Actually, don't look to them for your own awakening, ever. Notice how they participate in the world after their awakening, and watch for what costume they decided to put back on. Many Mystics are bringing back some of the old rituals, traditions, and techniques, recreating them and using them to function in this three-dimensional reality. Again, though, they know that none of it is reality. Even at that, the people looking to them for their own awakening will see what they are doing and think that their current actions comprise the path to awakening. This is a false idea. This is just the awakened person's costume. It fits the person perfectly, and it won't fit anyone else.

Awakening only comes from the inside. It can never come from a person, place, or thing. It can never come from a teaching, idea, or practice. With that in mind, why even write this type of book? I'm pointing to the moon. Feel the words, go inside, and see what happens within you. There is where you will find your reality.

GOING NOWHERE FAST

We seem to be constantly on the run. As we are going from Point A to Point B, people are driving and trying to get there as fast as they can, and in the meantime, their bodies are full of rage and anger because other people are not going fast enough or getting out of the way as quickly as desired. We are all going nowhere fast. It made me think of a story that I read somewhere about a man who went to another country to give a lecture. He was waiting for the train, and apparently, the train was just a few minutes late, so the man decided to take a cab because he was in such a hurry. This man needed to get to the lecture hall on time and he was so focused on the time that he decided that he didn't have a minute to spare. The man didn't even notice his surroundings. He had never been to this country before and he didn't notice where he was located. He was surrounded by beautiful architecture, old cobblestone roads, and cars going in a different direction than what he had known. He didn't notice any of these things! He jumped into the cab and asked the driver to go as fast as he could. The cab driver started to speed. The man was going through his notes for the lecture, and after a few moments, realized that he never gave the driver an address. He then asked the driver,

"Do you know where we are going?"

The driver said,

"No! But I'm going as fast as I can!"

I can see that this is how many of us live our lives every day. We're just going, going, going nowhere fast. We never seem to take note of where we are in the moment. We don't notice that there is a hawk circling overhead, we don't notice the changes in the trees as they anticipate the arrival of fall, and we don't notice that a sign was moved or that someone is walking along the side of the road. We don't notice these things because we're going nowhere fast. We're not in the present moment, for we're too busy trying to get to the next moment, and once we are in the next moment, guess what? We only want to get to the next one after that.

I have this experience every day. I used to do these things every day. My observations have me noticing how people are unaware of the current moment because they're trying to get to the next moment fast, and how where they are going is nowhere, because when the mind is constantly in the future of where you want to go and not in the now, you're not living. That is not living. It's getting to the next moment. It's just like the greyhound chasing the rabbit. Before the greyhound knows it, the race is over and he never gets the rabbit. Instead of being in this moment of time and realizing that this moment is all that we have, we go and go, and the next thing that we know, life has passed us by and we are in our last moments of life with regrets.

You are wasting this moment by trying to get to the next. Just be in this moment. If you are driving from Point A to Point B, take in your surroundings, notice the driver in front of you, and notice the person behind you. Notice how the person behind you is right on your bumper because they are trying to get nowhere fast. I just smile inside because that was me, and that is me. Pay attention to how your body is responding when you're trying to get from Point A to Point B. I live in the Chicago metro area, and to get anywhere, you have to drive. Public transportation in the area is, well, there is none. If I want to go to the grocery store, I have to get into my car to drive. I choose to get into my car. Being around people, like the guy who hopped into a taxi and went as fast as he could only to not get anywhere, can add a lot of stress to the body. We are living in heightened, stressful states. And these stressful states release chemicals in the body such as adrenaline and cortisol. Too much cortisol in the body can cause inflammation and thin the bones. Osteoporosis is one of the fastest-growing health issues in our country. We are living in a constant state of stress. These chemicals are constantly flooding our bodies, and we're creating inflammation and a bad situation in our physical bodies. Our bones are thinning by trying to handle the weight of our stress. We're creating an environment for our physical bodies that is not healthy.

The body is part of the mind, body, and spirit whole. Some people put too much focus on the mind, or too much focus on the spirit. Balance is key.

The physical body has a cycle of its own. My body is going through a healing cycle and I now allow it. The body is always seeking balance. Nature is always seeking balance. I am feeling my body heal, and it is such a beautiful process. In addition, I take full responsibility for the state that I put myself in for all of those years. That's awareness right there!

When I'm around a lot of people, I can feel their energy and chemical bodies in such heightened states that when I am surrounded by a lot of people, it can sometimes make me physically sick. I wondered if others who are in the awakening process also have similar experiences. Our energy and chemical bodies can influence others, and when I feel that along with the healing that I've been doing on myself, I start to become physically sick. The only way that I can describe it is that it's almost like an allergic reaction. At that moment, I'm having an allergic reaction to the people surrounding me.

I hear so many people say that they can't be around large groups of people. It made me wonder if this energy or chemical interaction is the reason why. Is this why others who have come to enlightenment hid themselves in the past? In our modern world, there is no place to hide. Go to places that make you feel good and soak in the environment. If you do go to places that have a lot of people, just be sure to ground yourself in the moment. Observe what is happening around you. Add some of the mystical techniques such as carrying a stone with you, like a small rose quartz, and have the intention that the energy that you use to absorb, the stone will now absorb. This is the way of the Modern Mystic, using techniques such as this one with intention.

WHO AM I?

How many times have you asked yourself, "Who am I?" Many of us will identify ourselves to what it is that we do. For example, I am a sign language interpreter, a massage therapist, a woman, and a mother. I do many different things, but the things that I do, do not define who I am. People will ask, "What do you do?" The ego is built within our language. I *am* an interpreter, I *am* a massage therapist, I *am* a mother, and I *am* a sister. It is our language that kind of feeds into that ego identification. These titles are not even tangible things. They are all illusory. I can't hold in my hand, "I am sister, I am wife, or I am mother," yet I identify myself with those illusory titles. Whereas now, I ask, "Who am I?" My answer is, "I am a perfect manifestation of consciousness. I am here in this experience, and then I allow my experiences to unfold."

Instead of asking, "Who am I?" Ask, "What do I experience?" I experience sign language interpreting, I experience being a mother, I experience being a wife, and I experience being a daughter. These are my experiences, but my experiences do not define who I am. I am a perfect manifestation of Source here having a physical experience. I wear many costumes. I can change my costume in an instant. In one instant, I'm a daughter. In the next, I'm a mother. Therefore, when I let go of attachments to those titles, I allow myself to fully experience those things. The question is no longer, "Who am I?" It's "What is my experience?" This is a shift of consciousness and awareness.

When we attach ourselves to these titles, we give our power over to them and allow them to define who we are. There may come a day when I am no longer an interpreter, or where I'm no longer a massage therapist. If I assign and attach myself to these titles, I may one day not do these things anymore; it could cause great suffering in the mind and body. It is the same idea when we attach ourselves to our physical things. Say that we have a car and become attached to it, and one day, experience an accident. The car is declared totaled. We're heartbroken for the car and this loss causes great physical stress. It's just a car! Cars can be replaced, but people can't in this reality. We not only have attachments to physical things, but many people will have attachments to the things that they do and experience.

When we give ourselves a title like, "I am a mother," we attach ourselves to a title and it's kind of like holding onto air. It's not real. I see many women hold onto, "I am a mother," and they allow it to define who they are. When the children grow up and become adults, they have a terrible time letting go of "I am mother." Some women will attach so strongly to being a mother that when their children grow up, they will still "mommy" their grown children. This action can cause great suffering in the mind and body.

A process that one can use is to keep asking, "Who am I?" No matter what comes up, write it down and then challenge it. Is that really who you are? When you no longer have attachments to the titles, what you realize is that you are everything. You are connected to everything around you. When we attach ourselves to a title like, "I am a mother," we limit ourselves from every other possibility of allowing that into our experience. Challenge those beliefs you have that you think define who you really are or who you think you really are. For any titles that you give yourself, challenge them. This process will start to open you up to possibilities and let you see more of what the universe might bring to your door. There was a time when I had no idea that I would ever become an author, ever. Yet when I opened myself up to possibilities, things just started happening, books just started pretty much writing themselves, and other opportunities started opening up. If I held onto, "I am an interpreter," that would have been it. This would define what I do and who I am. I would have closed off all of those doors that the universe was opening up for me. Then, when I realized that I am all of these things, that I am all of the possibilities, and that I am a perfect expression of Source, things started coming into my experience that I never dreamed possible.

When some people are studying spiritual teachings and philosophies, they can start to get hung up on the idea that none of this existence is real. This reality is an illusion. Someone who has seen and experienced realization will have limited words to express the experience. Let's say that someone has experienced realization and then said, "Well, it's all an illusion."

I've seen many people say this very thing. Many will hear this statement and hang onto the words and parrot, "Well, it's all an illusion." Yet in our physical realm, it's all very much real. You can touch the dog and the cat, and they can touch you. In this realm, it's very much real, but someone who has experienced awakening realizes that this concept is a very small part of the entire picture. Most of us see this physical realm as everything. That is the illusion. That is the illusion! That we are alluding ourselves to think that we are it, that this is it. That is the illusion! It's not that everything is an illusion. Realizing that there are other realms or dimensions above and beyond this reality is enlightenment. Again, words can confuse here, because saying above and beyond means something better than where we are right now. There is nothing better than where we are right now. This is the perfection. What we are constantly doing is looking for something else instead of being right where we are and being in that perfection. When you are constantly looking for something else, then where you are becomes illusory, because you are not where you are, you're constantly someplace else. As a result, there's a lot of talk about this reality just being an illusion. It's a misunderstanding.

We only feel, taste, and hear through our senses a very small amount of the bigger picture. What we perceive with our physical senses is just the tip of the iceberg. We don't have the capability to measure or perceive the entire bottom part of the iceberg. That is why when we see the tip of the iceberg, we say that it is reality. This is it. That is reality, for this is where we are. This is everything. Yet someone who has attained realization will see the entire iceberg and see that most people

look at the tiny tip and think that this is it. That's the illusion…
not that the tip of the iceberg is an illusion.

We can start to change our language by, instead of saying,
"It's all an illusion," start to acknowledge that we have limited
perception. Acknowledge the limits that we put on ourselves.
In the beginning, I did use the word *illusion*, but something
about the word didn't feel right. This is how I learned to express
it. That is how other people have expressed it. Yet we are here
in this physical reality, so logically, it's not an illusion. The truth
is that in the entire grand scheme of things, we have limited
perception. We cannot perceive the entire picture because our
limited physical senses don't allow us to do that. When we go
through the body's gateway into an entirely different realm,
we are able to perceive the entire iceberg, so to speak. Then
we are able to perceive the limited perceptions that we have in
this body. I think more and more of us are starting to realize
that there is no real way to express the experience in words.
However, as a Mystic, I'm trying to do just that. I'm attempting
to get a point across because there might be a combination of
words that I might use that triggers something in someone and
makes them say, "Yes! That is what I'm looking to do." All of a
sudden, their perception can open up a little bit more, and then
a little more, and then just a little bit more after that. I feel like
this is the reason why some people who experience realization
just kind of crawl into a cave and isolate themselves. They do
it because it's overwhelming. It's scary. It's a feeling of bliss and
fear at the same time. Then there are some who may be able
to put limited words to the experience so that someone else
can read it and say, "Oh my gosh, that's what I've been looking

for all along. That's the feeling that I'm feeling, and I can't put words, feelings, thoughts, or emotions to it." Why? Because when you experience this realization, there are no emotions that you can use to describe it. We can use the word *bliss*, but then we could use the word *terrifying* at the same time. Do you see? There is no duality when you have this experience. With our physical emotions, there is always duality. Physical emotions are measured in a linear way, through the stick analogy. In a linear fashion, we have depression or disempowerment at one end of the stick, and feelings of love and joy on the other end of it.

I'm not talking about those physical emotions. I'm talking about emotions that have no duality. They are one. When you have your experience, you will experience what you want to call bliss, but also what you want to call horror at the same time. That's the beauty of it! That's the illusion. That opens up your mind to the illusion and the duality that we have with our physical emotions. Then, we realize that our physical emotions are very much limited perception. When you come to realization, there is no limited perception. All is One. Again, using limited words, hopefully I've expressed it with some meaning, but then again, there is no meaning. That's the beauty of being a Mystic. At one point, I say one thing, and in the very next chapter, I say its opposite and that it's all true. It's all a perfect expression of consciousness.

PERCEPTION

I can share some of the practices that I did to expand my
perception and awareness. For every opportunity that I
could think of before my realization, and even now, when
I'm in the midst of the role that I'm playing, there have been
some moments when scenarios have seemed very real. In those
moments, I expand my awareness and perception. It's a simple
thing to do. My preferred example to use for explaining the
expansion of perception and awareness is driving a car. Most of
us have experienced driving. While driving the car and going
to work, most of us will turn on the radio and distract ourselves.
We won't even realize that there is a person driving behind us
or that there is a cop car in the median of the road a half of a
mile ahead. That hawk circling overhead? You bet we don't
notice that either. There is no perceiving or becoming aware
of these things. What I do, and still do, is turn off the radio.
To me, the distraction has become like nails on a chalkboard.
Instead, I perceive that I am the experience of everything in
my surroundings. I am the experience of the trees that line the
road, the telephone poles and the wires that connect them. I am
connected to everything. My perception of my surroundings

opens up. If there is an animal wanting to cross the road, I can feel it before it happens, and I'm prepared. It could be a little squirrel, and I'll feel the experience of that little squirrel as a sentient being. It is an expression of consciousness, and it is perfection. I feel it before I see it with my eyes, and as I perceive it, I'm able to slow down so that the critter can cross the road safely.

Even for the case of the angry driver who cut me off on the highway, I would think to myself, "I am that person." If I was in a blind hurry to get somewhere, I might angrily cut someone off, too. Then I'm able to let go of it. With road rage, we can pick up another person's anger, and we almost enter into their state. It perpetuates this state of awareness or rather unawareness. Being connected to your states of awareness equals awakening. On a recent morning when I drove to work, it was early, the moon was up, and it was just beautiful. I sent feelings of love to the moon and I could feel love (energy) coming from it. I was the experience of the moon. I set my intention to allow myself to expand awareness and perception.

To expand my awareness, I imagine that there is this hoola-hoop ring around me, and it gets bigger and bigger and bigger. Start with it just a couple of feet off of the body, and just be aware of everything that is around you within that hoola-hoop ring. When you're ready, you can imagine the ring getting bigger and bigger and bigger. This is something that you feel or imagine. Close your eyes and really connect with the space within your hoop. I did a meditation once in which I imagined a hoola-hoop ring that encompassed the entire Earth. I felt as if I was one with the Earth. I was the experience of the Earth as a sentient being. These are things that you can do to train yourself, if you will, but again, don't make these practices 'it.' This example is not the only way. It is just one way to incorporate play with expanding your perception and awareness. Practice as if you have no expectations. You're just having fun with it, and then one day, you'll realize or feel like you are everything within your awareness, or within your hoola-hoop. Then, you'll begin to feel the trees, the individual grass blades, everything, and you'll experience everything within your perception. There are many other tools out there; this is just one of many examples that I used. By just noticing and becoming aware of the space in which you are in, you will become aware that you're not the only one, but you are the only one.

BECOMING ONE

Within our physical world, we are naturally drawn to each other. We will seek out that which compliments us. A perfect example is sex. We are drawn to each other on a chemical level. We are all created from that energy, from the sexual center, or what some call the second chakra, or the creative energy center of the body just above the pubic bone and below the belly button. We may have a strong desire to go back to that energy in order to become one. We have two separate people instinctively drawn to each other to become one. Within our language, we have a phrase of, "You complete me."

It can be a very physically orgasmic experience to which some become addicted. In this realm, we can only perceive our physical bodies with our physical senses, but we also have our energy body that many of us cannot sense. We are constantly being drawn to become one with this consciousness, or source. In the physical realm, we are always being drawn toward the sexual orgasmic experience; in the spiritual realm, we are constantly searching for the orgasmic spiritual experience. Shamans will use herbs to open up the pineal gland so that those who want to connect with spirit can have that experience.

Payote and Ayawaska are examples of herbs that shamans will use to assist in the spiritual experience. However, we do not need them to have the experience. We are all drawn to become one with God. You don't need anything outside of yourself to have a spiritual experience. Once you have the perception that you are not separate from God, there is no longer a need to seek.

When you let go of beliefs that limit you, you will begin to open up to more and more of these spiritual experiences. You are opening yourself up to realization. Once you experience realization, you can have a spiritual orgasmic experience just by looking at a kitten or another person's face. There's the difference. I know a lot of people might say, "Oh my gosh, I had this experience; therefore, I must be enlightened." You just opened up the window a little bit more, and that's great! Keep opening up a little more and a little more. I can't tell you how many spiritual experiences I had before I disappeared. There were many. Each time, I could feel this opening up inside. It was never the same as the realization experience. That was like…I don't know how to explain it. It was complete. Some of the spiritual experiences, I can explain. They were "smaller" comparatively.

Your physical body is constantly looking for that physical experience of orgasm. Our spiritual or energy body is always on the lookout for that spiritual orgasm. That's why a lot of us are seeking. We are seeking for the truth. We are constantly seeking for that experience or that one piece of truth. The thing is, that piece of truth is not one piece of truth. It's everything. Everything! When you allow that, you no longer feel the duality.

I think that's the difference between spiritual experiences and the realization experience. There is no separateness; there is no duality. With spiritual experiences, you come back and you're right back into that duality. Once you attain realization, there is no more duality. You can play many different roles and have fun in the physical experience. Someone is telling you one thing, and you can see and bring out the opposite side to help them realize that both options are true. That's what I do. What happens? I piss a lot of people off, because what they are looking for is someone to side with them. That is ego. Everyone has an agenda, and you see right through that agenda. I'm on both sides. Someone says, "Oh we shouldn't be a socialist country or we shouldn't be this or we shouldn't be that." Yet if you think about it, we are all of those things. If you look at the whole, you begin to see and become aware in the mind. The mind starts to accept this non-duality.

It helps to understand the differences between spiritual experiences, and then the experience of realization or awakening. I had many spiritual experiences, but it was the realization that opened my eyes. How does one explain the difference? I would ask myself these types of questions while writing this book. I'd leave it alone for a day or two, and all of a sudden, a picture would pop into my head. An example popped into my head when asking about what words to use to explain the difference. That's the thing with awakening; there are no words, only metaphors.

My daughter and I took a class and learned how to shoot a rifle. We learned about how to be safe and properly use a rifle. Then, we got to do some target practice. I shot off several rounds, shooting at this piece of target paper several yards away. I could see how one shot would put a hole in the target paper, and I could barely see through it. After several rounds, however, I was able to break through the target, and when I retrieved my target paper, I could see right through it, because shooting in the same area created this big hole in the target paper.

The visual that I received for comparing spiritual experiences to awakening is that when we have these smaller spiritual experiences, we start to break through that veil, if you will, the veil of the ego, that keeps us closed off and separate from source. Each one of those spiritual experiences will shoot another hole through that veil, and with more and more spiritual experiences, you will shoot enough holes in it to eventually, completely, break through that veil. That's what I felt like when I was going through my experiences. I had many spiritual experiences, and I've even experienced what is called a sacred healing with a shaman from South America. What that experience did for me was thin out that veil even more, so that I could eventually break right through that which was gradually, already, becoming weaker and thinner. It's not something tangible onto which you can hold.

Our ideas and beliefs that we are separate will thicken that veil; make it stronger. The belief that I'm sitting here, and you're over there and that we are separate from each other will reinforce the veil. Our beliefs that we need to have things a certain way with money, economy, or what have you, really help to strengthen that veil. Our ideas and beliefs in a political structure or religious structure strengthen that veil. If you want the veil to become thin and eventually break through, you must start breaking down or shooting through those beliefs.

Start to break down those beliefs. What are they? From where do they come? Do I believe in them? It was Jesus, Buddha, and many of the spiritual leaders who have said, "Don't believe anything that I tell you; test for yourself." What may be true for me in my experience, may not be true for you. You may have a different experience. You may have a sudden awakening. You may never wake up in this lifetime. What is important is that you just be right where you are. If you never wake up...so be it. You are still going to seek because it's in us to seek to find that balance between the physical and spiritual. That is why many of us are seeking. We are all seeking for answers, seeking for that spiritual orgasmic experience. When you are awake, your world inside is seeking expression and experience. Those that are not awake yet, will look outside themselves for answers.

Many of us will go to inipis or sweat lodges, drumming, church, and participate in chanting or ritual, or whatever we are drawn to for that ultimate spiritual experience. The reason why we go to these things is because of the connectedness to the spiritual realm that they give us. That is what it is that we are wanting. It's not the things that we do that are important; it's the feeling of doing those things that is important to us. The more that you can achieve that feeling and allow yourself to experience, the more you'll start to thin the veil. It doesn't matter what path you take. You can follow the path of the Buddha, and that would be fine. You can follow the path of Jesus. That's also fine. Either choice does not equate to the ultimate path. Just use their paths as an example of a guide. Just like the image of the hand pointing to the moon, it's guiding you to see the moon. You can make up your own path, and that is probably best. Take a little of this and a little of that. Take some of what the Buddha taught, some of what Jesus taught, and some of what Osho taught, or whatever you are drawn towards, and make your own way. That is best. What feels right for you? The point is, you need to begin to thin the veil or shoot enough holes in it to weaken it in order to open you up to realization. It can be done.

I believe that this was something that I was searching for since I was a teenager or earlier. Coming from the background from which I came, I started seeking, and I learned so much head knowledge. It was only when I started to challenge the ideas in my head and everything that I learned, that I started to weaken the veil. I embraced them, and then let go of them. Then, I allowed myself to have more spiritual experiences. The veil became thinner and thinner. Learning to shoot a rifle was one of my many joyful experiences that I shared with my daughter; I would have never guessed that the experience could be used as a metaphor for awakening!

SEPARATION OF
YIN AND YANG

When we are in spirit form, there is no separation, but as soon as we come to this physical form, our physical bodies create a split. In spiritual form, the mind and spirit are not divided at all. Yet as soon as we come into physical form, we create this duality. We separate the mind from the spirit. Scientists can't really pinpoint exactly where the mind is located. Some people think that it's in the brain. The brain has a lot of functions; however, the mind is not in the brain. The mind is encompassed within the entire body. We even express this notion in our language. For example, we might say, "I have a gut feeling." That feeling sends signals to the brain to put words to that gut feeling. You may experience a feeling in the heart. You may have experienced a broken heart. The feeling comes from the heart, but it sends signals to the brain in order to put words to it so that you can deal with it or express it on a physical level.

I thought about the yin and yang symbol. Mind and spirit are one, but as soon as we come into this physical realm, the body separates or creates this duality of separating the mind and spirit. If you look at the yin and yang symbol, mind being on one side and spirit on the other, that line that divides the one into two is the body. That can be a visual of mind, body, and spirit. The three aspects of one. When we connect the mind and the body, or awaken to what we originally were, that's awakening, going back to our original state while in the physical. Many of us, sometimes as soon as we are born, are seeking to go back to that feeling of oneness. That is why we seek pleasures, religious experiences, desires, and spiritual attainment.

When we have our experience of enlightenment, we remember everything from when we, as the creator, source, universe, or whatever you want to call it, agreed to separate. We had to detach in order to create and experience in this physical realm. This separation had to happen in order to start the creation process in this physical realm. The separation is the yin and yang. It's opposing forces working together in order to create. As a result, source disconnected from itself. That was the beginning of the creation, starting with yin and yang. We, in this physical experience, comprise the extreme opposite in consciousness of the creator. The creator is the yang, the giver, and we, in this physical form, equal the exact opposite, yin. We are the receivers of this creation. It's something to which we agreed, something that we had to do, but in order to experience this separateness, we had to create mind in this physical world so that when we observe the food that we eat, we can see that which is good and that which is bad. It allows us to take delight in experiences that we can enjoy. With that enjoyment in this physical realm, we can also experience its opposite. We are the opposite; we created the opposite, so we've come full circle.

That is the definition of this shift, a going back to the creator, and this is why many of us are feeling that shift in consciousness and that desire to come to realization. The realization is the memories that start coming, and it starts in the heart. It really does not start in the mind. It is our heart that feels like something is missing. That's why seekers seek; they are looking for something, but they don't quite know what it is. They are looking with their minds. Instead, begin to look with your heart. It's not going to be found in any religion, because religions are designed to keep you seeking. They are designed to keep on the veil. It's part of the process, having this veil that we put on. It's part of the agreement, the arrangement that we made as soon as we separated from the creator, source, God, all that is energy. Just like everything is created with energy, everything in this physical realm is energy, but in order for us to enjoy it, to have desires, we had to disconnect. It's all perception. Perfection.

GIVE AND RECEIVE

Giving is yang and receiving is yin. We are the yin, the receivers, the opposite extreme of source. Source gives, while we receive. We are the ones who will receive something from source and call it good, receive it openly, and thank God. Yet when we receive something that we label as bad, we close ourselves off from it, and blame God. In linear, dualistic thinking, the two ends of the stick, we are on one end of the stick and source is on the other. That is the split from source. At one time, we were one, a circle if you will, and then we split off from source, creating a linear line. When you bring the two ends together, you have one circle. One.

Be open to receiving everything. Remind yourself that it is our human linear thinking that labels it as good or bad, but it was still something that was given so we should receive it openly. If I were to give my friend a gift, and she loved it, then I would feel joy in the giving. Or, if I was to give something to someone and they hated and rejected that gift, I would feel rejected. This is a linear pattern with our giving and receiving. Source does not feel rejected; we just receive more of what we send out. We receive everything from the universe. This yin and yang balancing act is just that: It is a constant balancing. Nature only knows balance. When things are out of balance, she gets to work with finding that balance. As a result, we create this imbalance, and nature is constantly seeking balance. Yet we blame God for what it is that we are receiving. This is the universal law of cause and effect.

We do things without ever considering the effect. We will experience an effect and think, well, this must be God's will. It's not. We are the opposite extreme of God. This is one of the laws of the universe at work. There are many laws of the universe, or forces at work, all of the time. Within our physical realm on Earth, we have gravity. Within our physical universe, there have been forces, or universal laws, set up and we are constantly working against them. Those laws don't care about our ignorance. We know about the law of gravity, so we don't jump off of buildings. Yet there are these other laws that are at work that we ignore or don't realize exist.

If we drill for oil, something that we caused, there is going to be an effect. We might not see it right away, but in this lifetime, we are starting to see the effects of previous generations before us. We now know the effects of the things that we used to do, what they can cause, what they can do, and their dangers. Yet we are only seeing these changes because the effect cycle had already started. Now, nature is trying to balance what we've done, so all that we see is the effect. We don't take into consideration the cause. We might not even see the cause, but we are only seeing the effect, and therefore, it must be God. We will blame God and call it, "An act of God," rather than an effect of our causes, or what we did to cause this situation.

It may have been a cause from years ago, and we are just now seeing the consequences of it.

I've read about a tribe of Indians that valued cause and effect. Before they would do anything, they would sit down and discuss what the possible effects were in five or more generations out. If they felt that there were any negative effects five generations out, they would not do it. In the present, we only consider how much we're going to make and how much we're going to profit from it. We don't consider the effect that it will have on our children, our grandchildren, and our great-grandchildren.

There is only one universal mind, and that is consciousness. I shouldn't say mind because that can be confused with our human-thinking ego mind. I mean mind in how things work and the intelligence that is behind the very first separation. It's that mind to which all of us are connected because we are that mind. We are the opposite extreme. That is why many of us will feel, let's not use the word *shame*, but a sense of *discord*. We feel the discord of the separation. It feels like something is missing. That's it. There is something missing, and it's the other part of us from which we are cut off. Yet we are whole, so we are constantly seeking because of that empty feeling.

For anything that we ask, source gives and we receive. Even the Bible says, "Ask, and you shall receive." When we ask for something, the other part of ourselves will give it to us. It will happen even if we ask for things that we don't want, and that happens all of the time. We will think about the things that we don't want to experience, yet they'll manifest in our experience. We don't want wars, yet our world is full of them. Rather than thinking about what you don't want to experience, think about what you do want in your experience. All experiences will be happening within our reality because this is what we asked for at the time. We could not experience these things in our original form. We had to separate. Therefore, in order to experience what we do every day, what we experience, whether we label it as good or bad, we had to separate. We couldn't experience these things in our original form, so that feeling of something missing, when you realized what it was that was missing, that we were separate, the empty feeling, that empty space, was what we had to create. If we did not, there was no way that we could have filled it with the physical experiences of this realm.

As for that empty vessel, well, we are the vessel and that emptiness is source. That is realization. It hits when you realize that we were originally a circle and that this is a metaphor, when we were, at one time, one with source. Then, however, we cut that circle and made it a straight linear line. On one end of the stick, we have the positive, and on the other, the negative end of the stick. We have the yin on one end, and on the other end, the yang. Yet we are still source. When we come to realization, we bring the two ends of the stick together. There is no separation. It can be done while still in this physical body. Then, what we realize is that everything, *everything*, even at one time when I called some of my experiences horrific, has love in that experience.

I've been asked, "How can we all be one?" The analogy that I thought of is a hologram. I love science fiction, and the idea of a hologram came to me as an answer to this question.

You have one hologram that has an image imprinted on it. If you were to break that hologram into two pieces or two billion pieces, it wouldn't matter. If you were to shatter that hologram into however many pieces you picked, every single one of those pieces would have a piece of the original picture or imprint. That is why we are all one. We all come from the same source or imprint. We all have a piece of that original imprint. We are all imprinted with source, only we are a physical reality of that imprint and there is also the reality that we can't see.

What left the imprint is not from this physical world. It is from the spiritual world. Shamans and Mystics have all said that there are separate worlds, but we cannot perceive them with our physical senses. We, in our physical form, are able to live in this physical world because we have our five senses that perceive and have a perception of this physical dimension. Yet we also have the senses from which our physical senses were imprinted: the sixth sense. That sixth sense includes all of our senses and then some, but in the spiritual world. That means that we have five senses in the physical realm and hundreds of senses in the spiritual realms. We cannot perceive these senses in our physical bodies. We must go through the gateway in order to perceive them. That gateway is within you.

THE BODY IS YOUR GATEWAY

I've heard the saying, "Your body is a temple" for my whole life. I'm sure that most of us are led to believe that this saying has to do with the food that we feed our bodies. That is true to an extent. We are what we eat. It is important to feed the body clean food, but what is happening in our time has never happened at any other time in our history. We are modifying our food on the level of DNA. By genetically changing our food, we are genetically changing the human body. The vision that I saw during a meditation was the body being an actual temple, with a gateway or a door. It is this gateway in the heart area. In my meditation, it looked and felt like crystal. The body is an actual gateway to the higher realms. It is not something outside of the human body.

I do cleanse my body by juicing and eating high-nutrient dense foods, eating as cleanly as possible. I do have yummy foods in moderation. It is okay to have the treats, for isn't that why we come here for the experience? However, eating clean has helped de-muddy, if you will, that gateway to help me open the door to the spiritual worlds. I guess that there could be a couple of meanings to that saying, "Your body is a temple."

For surely, it is what we feed our bodies, and for me, what I fed my body for the last 40-something years has manifested itself as disease such as inflammation in the body, autoimmune disease, and cancer.

When I began eating living food, my body started to heal, and that gateway or temple door began to crack open. The importance of treating your body as a temple and feeding it the best possible food and feeding it the best possible thoughts that you can is clear to me. There are some who will say that it really doesn't matter. They will try and convince themselves that if they eat a Twinkie and think positive thoughts that the Twinkie will not do damage to the physical structure of the body. The chemicals and high-sugar content won't cause a chemical reaction from the pancreas if they just think positive thoughts. There are forces at work in the body that are beyond the thoughts in our mind. The body has its own consciousness, and when we see the body as a temple and give it the honor and respect that it rightly deserves, it in turn will treat us the same way. As a result, our experience in this physical realm will be one without dis-ease. Eating clean has made a difference in having a clear opening in the temple.

Some of us will have limited access to all organic food. It's interesting that we have to categorize organic food with regular food. It should really be the other way around. We have food, and then we have Franken-food. Many don't have access to real food because of where they live or not being able to afford to spend the money on organic food. The important thing is to make the best choices that you possibly can in your area in what you feed your body. I know a lot of people in poorer areas, especially in urban city areas, will say that they can get a fast-food meal for $4, but for a week's worth of $4 fast-food meals, you can also get a bag of rice, a bag of beans, and some olive oil. It will take some adjustment in your taste buds and in your mind because of the conditioning that you allowed yourself, but you can make a whole week's worth of beans and rice to feed a family. Make up all of the excuses that you want, but it's only mind. You are basically making up your limitations.

There are always choices that we can make to treat the body as a temple and remembering that this body is a gateway to the spiritual realm. It's not anything outside of you. Nothing outside of you can open that gateway to the spiritual world. It is your body. Your body is the door; it is the first entryway into the spiritual realm. Become connected with your body, love your body, and see it as the miracle that it really is, for that is a vitally important part of our spirituality.

In contrast, I've met and seen a lot of people who are so into their spiritual side, but their bodies are falling apart, literally. They only get so far with their spiritual studies and they don't understand why they are not progressing further. It is because they're looking for teachings and practices outside of themselves, whether it would be the teachings of a guru, tarot readings, akashic record readings, bodywork, or that latest and greatest technological gadget that's come out. I did these things myself until I made the connection that it wasn't those things, it was something inside of me that allowed me to open up and connect. The next thing that I knew, that door was cracked open and a lot of things started happening with me spiritually. There is nothing wrong with tarot readings and such, for they can offer great insight. If you are drawn to them, use them as a tool to go inside. Whenever I do a spiritual reading for someone, I am guided to get them into their body during the reading. This is a wonderful place to start.

You cannot separate the physical body from your spiritual self while trying to attain or reach awakening or enlightenment. You must see the physical body as a vessel. Within that vessel is the empty space. Go into that. Don't fill it with anything. Don't fill it with beliefs or ideas, new shoes, a new man or woman, or moving to a different location. Don't fill it with anything. Keep it empty, because that is the crack in the door and it is what will connect you to the higher spiritual realm. Again, I don't want to use the word *higher*, because higher sounds like it must be better. That is ego. It's not better; it connects you to the other worlds and opens up connection to your higher self. You are already connected.

Your body is a temple, literally, an actual temple. Treat it as such with the air that you breathe, the water that you drink, the food that you eat, and the thoughts that you think. The thoughts that you think feed your subconscious mind, and your subconscious mind doesn't know right or wrong. It doesn't know past or future, for it only knows right now. There is a lot out there about the Law of Attraction and the thoughts that you think and how they affect you. If you change your thoughts, you can change your experience in this physical world, which is a powerful step toward awakening.

GO INTO THE DARK

I have started to observe what others have come to realize, and it's been wonderful to see. Observing without judgment is such a beautiful, difficult thing. What I'm seeing is people talking about the light, allowing the light, and seeing the light as the way to awakening or attainment. That might be true for some, but from my experience and realization, it was diving headfirst into the dark. Go into the darkness. When we embrace the darkness, it can have no hold on us. For most of us, that darkness is in the subconscious mind. For me, this was a process that was very important to my awakening. Once you open yourself up and shed light on the dark, you open your consciousness to another level of experience. There are no fears. When we just allow in the light and suppress the dark, the darkness just retracts and will rear its ugly head when we least expect it.

I have met many who call themselves *lightworkers* and are afraid of the dark, and dark entities, as they call them. Those dark entities are within them, their own subconscious minds. It's their dark trying to surface, and unless we embrace it, love it, and release it, only then we can allow in more light.

We all have experiences throughout our lives, and some of them we may label as horrific. For example, someone may have had a traumatic experience such as rape; as a result of this experience, the person may have suppressed their emotional experience and now may have a fear of men or of getting raped again. We experienced something that we labeled as bad, and it is what will stop us emotionally from moving forward because of the suppressed emotions within our subconscious minds. Please understand that I'm not saying that rape is not bad. If we experience something, anything, without dealing with the emotions, we are only hurting ourselves. Yet if we can go into our subconscious and connect with that monster that it created in our subconscious mind and release it, then we will be free from the emotional attachment to the experience. However, most of us will suppress it for all of our lives and never choose to be free of the damage that it can do to us on a physical level.

This is one of the most difficult things to do. When our subconscious is filled with suppressed emotions and memories, it requires a lot of energy to keep those emotions suppressed. Some of us call that *baggage*. I like to call these types of suppressed emotional experiences *beachballs*.

Imagine if you will, beachballs, and trying to hold a bunch of them under the water. The beachballs represent our suppressed emotions, and the water represents the subconscious. If a person has never dealt with suppressed emotions, then they can be holding down a lot of beachballs! Even just one big, bad beachball can require a lot of energy to keep it down. These beachballs will try to come up to be dealt with once in a while. As soon as they do, we push them back down with eating, shopping, sex, drugs, or whatever else a person uses to distract oneself from dealing with the beachball that is trying to surface.

If we can somehow go deep inside and not be afraid of the emotions that are trying to surface, but embrace them, love them, and allow them to expand within us, then we can allow the expansion to get bigger and bigger. This can be a very frightening process, but if you can allow this energy to expand and get bigger, it will eventually release. The feeling that you get in the body is of pure bliss once that energy is released. Now, you will still have the memory, but you won't have the emotional attachment of that memory. The energy is released. The example that I like to give is the first time that I saw the movie *Halloween*, when I was in 8th grade. I was scared to death the first time I saw it, but by the 17th time that I watched the movie, it was almost funny. There was no reaction of fear. As you can see, you're releasing that energy, and you're no longer fearful of it. The suppressed fear of it creates shame and guilt. Once it is released, you will be able to talk openly about your experience without the shame or guilt connected to it. This is part of the awakening process, because in order for you to create a space to allow in the light, you have to go into the darkness. You must go into the darkness. Well, you don't have to do anything. This is just one way to release the energy so that energy can be freed and used for a higher purpose: spiritual awakening.

YOUR INTENTION
PAVES YOUR PATH

There is a lot of talk about intention these days. When you set an intention, you start things in motion energetically. Our intention is more powerful than most of us realize. From a Mystic's point of view, when you set an intention, you are summoning universal forces. How we use intention is really important. Most of us will set an intention using ego. When ego sets an intention, it has an agenda, which is basically, "What's in it for me?" The intention has to give ego some kind of benefit. From a Mystic's viewpoint, when we set an intention, it's usually for the good of all involved. There is nothing in it for me.

A simple example of setting an intention can be used when you leave for work in the morning. You set the intention to arrive safely. That is an intention for just the self. But from a Mystic's view, we add for the good of all involved. For example, this morning, I set the intention for myself to arrive to work safely, and it included not hitting any animals, not hitting any people, and not getting into an accident, with the end result intended to be a productive employee for the good of the company. Now that is a bigger intention than setting the intention that I arrive safely just for my own good. There is nothing wrong with including yourself in the safety, but if you keep your intention small, the results will be small. Yet if you expand the perception of your intention and include everything within the intention, and obviously you can't think of everything, but you add into the intention anything that you haven't thought of which would be for the good of all, then you have expanded the intention. I know that's a lame example, but from a Mystic's point of view, we do things not from our own agenda. Everyone has an agenda, but that is starting to shift.

I try to think about what my intention is with this book. It's to get the information out there. I could talk to one person at a time, but by writing a book and using my own financial resources to publish it, I have the intention that this book will get into the hands of those who are searching for it.

I open myself up to not just the United States, but anywhere in the world, and perhaps, someday, this book being translated into other languages. I set my intention to reach out to as many people who are searching. I feel that there are a lot of people searching for answers to this shift in consciousness that we have all started. Many of us feel it happening. I'm setting my intention to more than just me, but then, there is only me. I don't have the intention to make money, even though paying my bills is always nice, but I always find a way to pay my bills and live within or below my means. So please, share this book as much as possible. If you read it and you get something out of it, please share it with someone else who you think might benefit from it. There is a basic intention. The intention is set for not only me to benefit from it, but for others as well. Expand our intention.

We can limit ourselves with our intentions. In the movie, *The Secret*, it talks about asking for desires such as a fancy red car. For example, if I really want a fancy red car and think positively enough that I will get a red car, the universe will provide me with said fancy red car. Yet then we're closing the door on all of the other possibilities that the universe has to offer us. We can expand our intentions by asking, "Universe, I need a reliable car to get me to and from work dependably, I need it to be environmentally friendly, and something that the whole family can use." Therefore, I'm setting my intention not only for me just wanting a fancy red car so that I can look good in it and see other people looking at me in it, but instead, I'm opening up and including in my intention my family, my job, that I can arrive to work dependably, and including the environment so that it is environmentally friendly and not a gas hog. This is a more inclusive intention. I include all of those things, but at the same time, I'm opening myself up to a lot more possibilities. It's the same principle with any of our intentions. We have our wants and desires, desires to have a reliable, dependable environmentally friendly car, but then we also have our intentions that we can include and expand within our intention, and with that expansion, the universe opens up so much more for us.

Most of us, not all of us, from what I can see in the heart area, have a desire for this shift in consciousness to happen. We're ready for it. There are some people who don't have that area of the heart and fill themselves with fear. Fear will close you off to the possibilities. You will only see the fearfulness within everything. Set your intention to open yourself up to the possibilities of this shift that is happening. Is 2012 the end of the world? If it is, so be it. If it's not, so be it. It really doesn't matter from a Mystic's point of view. What matters is right now. What are you doing with right now? What kind of signals are you sending out to the universe, right now? What intentions are you setting right now? What desires do you have and want to fulfill right now? Do you have intentions and desires to want to fulfill only the ego? Or are you including Mother Earth? Are you including all sentient beings that reside on this Earth and call this planet home? Feel the difference?

From a Mystic's point of view, we are all one. Of course, I did and do have egoistic intentions and desires. And I will stop and ask myself questions to connect with my path. Is this going to hurt anyone else? Is what I'm intending just for my own desires and pleasures? Or, can I include the environment? Can I include other people in my desire and intention? Sometimes, when I have desires and intentions for my own gratification and ego, I may set them aside until I can come up with a way to include the greater good. That is what a Mystic will do.

I know that some pagan philosophies will teach that when you create a spell or intention, whether you call it a good spell or a bad spell, whatever you create and send out to the universe will come back to you stronger. Those who practice magic, spells, and intentions, are very careful with the spells that they create. If I cast a spell, I must be careful and ask, "How is this spell going to come back to me stronger? If I create a spell that is intended to hurt someone, the idea is that the spell will come back to me stronger than when I sent it out. If you have a desire or a thought of someone else failing, that will come back to you stronger, and you will be the one who will fail. Yet if you send out an intention for someone else to be successful, healthy, and experience abundance, that desire and intention will come back to you, stronger. You want to send out desires and intentions for others that they are successful and have abundance, and then it can come back to you without ego.

Let's say that I send out an intention that I have success and abundance. This intention is only for ego. That will fade or be short lived. You might get a little bit for a little while, but just as quickly as it comes, it will be gone. However, if you send out an intention and desire for someone else to be successful and have abundance, that intention will come back to you without ego. I don't know if I'm making myself clear with the difference. When you feed ego, it's very short lived. When you feed the universe, it goes on forever.

Part of being awakened and being a Mystic is being in both worlds. We are here in this physical world, and we are also in the various spiritual worlds. There is more than this world here that we can see, feel, hear, touch, and taste. There is a whole lot more that we cannot perceive. We walk the line between the worlds. Sometimes, we are more in the physical world, and sometimes, we're more in the spiritual world. In the way of the Modern Mystic, we are finding and creating our own path. That is what I mean by The Way: It's about finding your own path.

My path as a healer uses various techniques that I've studied. I choose to study the ways of shamanism, bodywork, nature spirits, kabbalah, energy work, and whatever else I am drawn towards learning and using. I take these teachings and then make them my own, knowing that my intention is probably the most powerful thing in using these teachings, theories, and philosophies as a healer. For someone who has seen or awakened, you know that none of this information really matters; I know that this is a projection from within. When people come to me needing healing, I create a space for healing. I will listen to them, feel them, and be with them as if I am them, because it is very real to them in this moment, and what I think doesn't matter. It is my intention to create a space for healing to happen and that is probably the most powerful aspect of my healing.

One of my personal favorite therapies to work with is cranial-sacral therapy. I love working the bones of the vertebra, the bones of the skull and the sacrum, the spinal fluid, the nervous system, and all of the soft tissue that attaches to the bones. Cranial-sacral therapy works with the nervous system, the spinal fluid and the meninges membrane, the membrane that covers the brain and the spinal cord. When I have someone on the table, it is important that I do not have judgments and that I keep my intention clear. My intention is for love, appreciation, and being in the moment with that person. Just with that and the human touch, it is very healing. I know that healing can only come from the inside, but when someone comes to me, I am there for that person and remind them to go inside and connect with their own body.

Others who have come to awakening might choose a different path. Maybe some who have awakened might choose a path of chiropractic, shamanism, or herbs and nutrition, writing or art. Know that it doesn't matter what path you choose. Pick one that matches your intention. My intention is to connect from the inside out. Therefore, when I make that connection within myself, I make that same connection within others. That heart space within me is the same heart space within the other person. When I make the connection, healing has already begun.

Some will choose to bring back the mythology and metaphors that we have inherited from a time that no longer serves us, and will create mythology and metaphors of our modern time by which we can live. Take, for example, the metaphor of when flying, if the oxygen masks come down, you put yours on first and then help the person next to you. That has become a metaphor of our time: to take care of yourself first so that you can be there for your loved ones.

Connect with your authentic self. This is something that most of us have to unbury. Many of us have never known that authentic self. It is something that comes from deep within that guides and gives inspiration. It is what Joseph Campbell said as, "Follow your bliss."

Choose whatever path you are drawn towards with the intention to help and heal others, and hopefully to spark something within them to awaken them to their own way. On the path of the way of the Modern Mystic, what is in the material world doesn't matter. It is all One. Just pick a path that feels right. Whatever you are drawn towards that matches your intention is what becomes your way.

I've learned several different healings and philosophies, and I pick and choose from each of the teachings that I learn. I may combine cranial sacral, energy work, and some shamanistic practices to create healing. You can combine the different lessons that you learn. Create your own path, because it does not matter what path you choose, for there is no right or wrong way. The point is to follow your intention. What is your intention for coming into this physical realm? What is our intention for being here? It's to connect so that we can bring each other up and heal each other. That is the way of the Modern Mystic.

Some people are bringing back the old practices and making them new again. Some of the pagan and Eastern practices and rituals have powerful meaning, but some of the meaning has been lost. There are those who are bringing those things back with meaning for our time to be reborn in our day of conscious awareness.

The Mystic perceives the different worlds. We know that there are different dimensions that we cannot perceive in this reality. In this reality, I perceive it as the heaviest reality with the most mass. Some shamans and Mystics will talk about the upper worlds or the higher worlds and levels within the spiritual worlds, not meaning better, but lighter, thinner, and having no mass. The spiritual worlds have less mass, dimension, and weight, and our physical bodies cannot enter these spiritual worlds. When they say the upper worlds, think of a balloon becoming lighter and lighter and being able to float upwards because it's so light that it defies gravity. That is what I mean by upper worlds. When journeying into these worlds, we go through the body.

There are worlds that we cannot perceive; we don't have the technology or the senses to perceive them yet. We do have some senses that we have not trained, and many of us are starting to train those perceptions. Most know it as the sixth sense, but it's not just one sense. Once you experience the upper worlds, you will notice that you have a lot more senses in the upper worlds. In this physical world, we have five senses, but when you experience the upper worlds, you have a lot more senses than just our five. The five senses that we have in this physical world are not able to perceive the non-physical.

Part of the way of the Modern Mystic is finding your path or way and training yourself to use your perceptions in the upper worlds and bringing that information back to this reality and then putting words to it. It is a challenge, because the only thing that we can liken it to is allegories, myths, or metaphors. We can only relate it to what we already know or have experienced. It will give others who are seeking a direction to look with what it is that we have perceived. It kind of gives them the experience of looking at the moon instead of at the hand pointing to the moon.

AFTERWORD

Since the first book was released, *Embrace the BITCH Within – Being In Total Connection with Herself,* many wonderful opportunities started to open up and more and more people started asking for more.

I knew I was going to write the third book *Rúnda 3 – Healing Through the Three Levels of Consciousness,* but I did not realize how important this work would be for so many.

Rúnda 3™ is practitioner system for Mystics, Healers and Urban Shamans that is used to heal, energetically balance, understand human behavior from the energy body's viewpoint, and to awaken and develop psychic or intuitive skills. The intention of Rúnda 3 is to bring you to your own conclusions and realizations.

This work has developed into a two day workshop and it is currently approved by the NCBTMB for 14 CE's for Certified and Licensed Massage Therapists. The response has been amazing!

I developed and designed *Rúnda 3 – Healing Through the Three Levels of Consciousness* for those in the healing arts to heal themselves and others, and to connect with their individual psychic gifts. When we learn how to use the 3 levels of consciousness and learn how they communicate, we open up to a deep level of healing ourselves and others, and opening up our individual intuitive/psychic gifts which can lead to your own realization or awakening.

By taking a Rúnda 3™ class, you will learn:
- What the Rúnda 3 symbol means
- The 3 parts of Consciousness
- The 3 parts of the Body
- How these are connected and how to use them
- The Energy Bodies and how they communicate
- The 3 part Breath
- How Rúnda 3™ is very different and beyond the teachings of the Law of Attraction
- The 3 step formula to manifestation
- How learning these steps leads to Psychic Development
- The 3 states of awareness
- The 3 steps of protection....and MORE!

Who would benefit from taking this class?
- All Lightworkers
- Reiki Practitioners (All Levels)
- Energy Healers of all backgrounds
- Anyone in the Healing Arts (i.e. massage therapists)
- Anyone interested in healing themselves and loved ones

Rúnda 3 is not for everyone, but if this resonates with you and you would like to learn more or would like to take a class or to have a class in your area, visit www.runda3.com.

REFERENCES AND RESOURCES

To learn more about Byron Katie and her books and workshops, visit her website at www.thework.com

Hendrix, Jimi. "The Star-Spangled Banner"

Byrne, Rhonda. The Secret. First edition. Atria Books/Beyond Words, 2006

Tolle, Eckhart. The Power of Now: A Guide to Spiritual Enlightenment. New World Library; 1ST edition (September 29, 2004)

To learn more about Cranial-Sacral Therapy, visit the Upledger Institute at www.upledger.com to find a practitioner in your area or to take a certification training.

To learn more about *Rúnda 3 – Healing Through the Three Levels of Consciousness*, please visit www.runda3.com

.

Made in the USA
Columbia, SC
02 June 2017